| DATE | | | |
|---|---|---|---|
| | | | |
| | | | |
| | | | |
| | | | |
| | | | |
| | | | |
| | | | |
| | | | |
| | | | |
| | | | |
| | | | |
| | | | |
| | | | |

# PET HAMSTERS

## Text and photos by JEROME WEXLER

Albert Whitman & Company   Morton Grove, Illinois

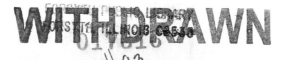

Also by Jerome Wexler
*Pet Gerbils*
*Pet Mice*

Library of Congress Cataloging-in-Publication Data

Wexler, Jerome.
     Pet hamsters / Jerome Wexler.
          p.   cm.
     Includes index.
     Summary:  Describes how to house, feed, and
     handle a pair of pet hamsters and the families
     they produce.
     ISBN 0-8075-6525-3
     1.  Golden hamsters as pets—Juvenile literature.
     [1. Hamsters.]  I. Title.
     SF459.H3W49    1992
     636'.3233—dc20                                    91-34914
                                                          CIP
                                                           AC

Text and photographs ©1992 by Jerome Wexler.
Published in 1992 by Albert Whitman & Company,
6340 Oakton Street,  Morton Grove, Illinois 60053-2723.
Published simultaneously in Canada by General Publishing, Limited, Toronto.
10 9 8 7 6 5 4 3 2 1

# Table of Contents

My first hamsters  5
What is a hamster?  6
Hamsters as pets  9
Golden hamsters and more  11
Before you buy a hamster  11
Get ready, get set...  12
Hamster housing  14
The waterer  14
Hamster workout  15
Keeping a hamster happy  16
The litter  16
What does a hamster eat?  17
Making a nest  19
No fleas, please!  20
Choosing a pet store  21
Decisions, decisions  21
Carrying home your prize  22
Getting to know your hamster  24
To wake a sleeping hamster  27
Keeping house  27
A healthy hamster  28

Choosing to have pups  29
Mating your hamsters  30
Preparing for the new family  32
The birth of the pups  32

*The Family Diary  35*
The pup's first day  35
Two days old  36
Four days old  36
Six days old  36
Seven days old  36
Nine days old  37
Ten days old  39
Twelve days old  39
Seventeen days old  40
Three weeks old  40
Four weeks old  41
Five weeks old  43

When a hamster dies  44
Photographing your hamster family  44
Index  47

## My first hamsters

"No! I don't want mice in the house. I simply won't have them!"

"But Mom, I want *hamsters*, not mice. And they're for school—they're going to be my science project for the year! I want a pair of hamsters so I can breed them and raise their babies. I'll pay for everything out of my allowance and I'll keep them in my room and I'll take care of them and I'll feed them and you won't even know they're around!"

This conversation took place many years ago, and what do you think happened? Well, you're right. I did get my hamsters. And guess who paid for the cages, the food, and the cute pair of hamsters? That's right—my mom.

I remember there was no school that day, so Mom and I went shopping at the pet store. I told the clerk that I wanted a pair of hamsters so I could breed them.

5

She said that adult hamsters are loners. That is, a hamster doesn't like having another animal in its cage. So if I wanted to buy two animals, I would have to buy two of everything—two cages, two waterers, two exercise wheels. I didn't expect that. While I had some money with me, it was not enough for two of everything! But my mom is the greatest, and without my even asking, she volunteered to pay for it all.

As I said, this happened years ago. I've since raised and bred a lot of hamsters, and I'd like to share with you some of the many things I've learned.

### What is a hamster?

Hamsters are small, gentle, clean animals with big black eyes and soft coats. They're inexpensive, easy to care for, and usually live long, disease-free lives. Best of all, they are gentle companions whose humorous antics are fun to watch. What more could one ask for in a pet?

Hamsters, like human beings, belong to a large group of animals called *mammals*. Both hamsters and humans are warm-blooded, grow hair, and produce milk for their young.

Scientists place hamsters, squirrels, mice, rats, beavers, chipmunks, and many other animals into the group of mammals called *rodents*. All members of this group, or order, have one thing in common—their front teeth grow constantly throughout their lives. Otherwise, each rodent is quite different. For example, mice and rats have long tails that are almost completely free of hair. Squirrels have long tails covered with lots of long hair. Beavers have long, flat tails covered with short hair. And hamsters have hardly any tail at all.

Various types of wild hamsters are found around the world, but the type that is most often sold in pet shops is the golden hamster, sometimes called the Syrian golden hamster. In 1930, Professor I. Aharoni found a mother hamster and her

babies in a desert in Syria. It is believed that all of today's pet hamsters came from three of those babies, a male and two females, which were given to the Hebrew University in Jerusalem by Professor Aharoni.

Adult hamsters range from five to six inches long and weigh four to six ounces. The female is both larger and heavier than the male.

Like many animals, hamsters have a keen sense of smell. They identify people, other animals, and even food by odor, rather than by sight, as we do. Touch is also an important sense for hamsters. Helped by their sensitive whiskers, hamsters can find their way in the dark and can determine if they will fit into small spaces.

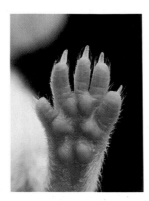

Hamsters' ears are almost always upright except when they are sleeping; then the ears are pulled back and lie flat. Hamsters have a good sense of hearing, although they may ignore any noise you make until you shake a box of hamster food. Sight is not as important to hamsters as the other senses.

Hamsters have rather small, flat noses, long whiskers, and long eyebrows. They have four toes on their front feet and five on their back feet. Hamster cheek pouches are especially interesting. Unlike our cheeks, which end at the back of our mouths, the cheeks of a hamster go all the way back to its shoulders! What's more, the pouch skin stretches, making each pouch into a voluminous storage area.

The rear legs of hamsters are larger and stronger than their front legs, but hamsters do walk on all fours. They often stand upright on their hind legs, looking like miniature bears, and like some bears, they use their front paws to hold and manipulate food.

Hamsters have loose skin on all parts

of their bodies. This makes lifting a hamster very easy. Just grab the skin between the shoulders and pick the animal up. In this area of its body, the skin can be pulled away as much as an inch.

### Hamsters as pets

Hamsters do make great pets, but they are not for everyone. You see, in their native desert habitat, hamsters avoid the heat by sleeping all day in their burrows and foraging in the cool of the early morning or late evening. So for hamsters, "morning" begins with our evening. If you want a pet to play with during the day, forget hamsters. However, if you spend most of your daylight hours away from home, a hamster may well be the perfect pet for you.

The eating habits of hamsters help make them easy to care for. Unlike many animals, hamsters do not immediately eat any food they find. When a hamster goes foraging (in the wild or in its cage), it fills its

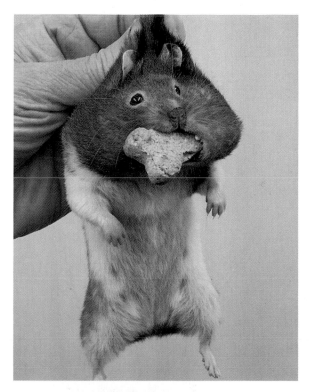

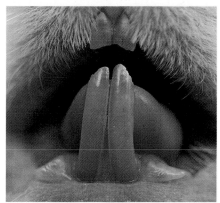

golden hamster

teddy-bear hamster

pouches and then returns to its nest, where it stores everything. It eats only what it needs at the moment. This hoarding habit makes it easy for your family to go away for a few days or even a week. Just leave a week's supply of food in the cage.

**Golden hamsters and more**

Although they are called golden hamsters, most hamsters found in pet shops are not golden but rusty brown. The tops and sides of their bodies are rust colored, and their undersides are mostly yellowish white. Their feet, both front and back, are pinkish and free of hair. This color pattern serves hamsters well in their native desert habitat. Their rusty-brown backs blend in with the color of the sand, protecting them from their enemies, while the whitish underside keeps them cool by reflecting heat given off by the sand.

In addition to golden hamsters, your pet shop may also have Chinese and Siberian hamsters. These two species are sometimes known as dwarf hamsters. They're about half the size of the golden hamster and not as friendly. Another, more rare species, is called the common hamster. Common hamsters are more than twice the size of goldens and usually have black bellies. They are also more aggressive and not often kept as pets.

Through years of breeding, golden hamsters are now available in several colors. They are also bred to have either long or short hair. The long-haired hamsters are known as teddy-bear hamsters and are quite popular. However, short-haired hamsters with rusty-brown coloring still outnumber the other varieties.

**Before you buy a hamster**

Before rushing off to buy a hamster, there are some things that you must consider. The life span of a hamster ranges from two to four years. Are you ready and willing to take on the care of an animal for this length of time?  Can you be totally responsible for its health and well-being?  And here's the toughest question:  are you willing to clean your pet's cage each week for the next one hundred to two hundred weeks?  That's a long time!  If the answer to any one of these questions is no, you'd better reconsider having a pet.  If the answer to every question is yes, then you are ready to talk to your family.

Bringing an animal into a house affects every person living there.  Is anyone allergic to animals?  Is anyone afraid of hamsters?  Does anyone object to your spending money on animals, equipment, supplies, and maybe vet fees?  Does everyone agree on where you will keep the hamster?  Is the family willing to take over the care and responsibility of your pet if you become ill or if you are away?  You should discuss these subjects with your family before you even visit a pet store.

There is just one more thing you should do before bringing home your hamster.  It is recommended that people who work with animals receive an anti-tetanus shot every few years.  Hamsters do bite, and a bite can lead to a disease called tetanus.  The germs that cause tetanus are found in such things as the dust that floats in the air, garden soil, and the feces of animals.  A bite from a hamster may do no harm by itself, but a deep puncture wound is a good place for tetanus germs to grow.  You should speak to your parents and doctor about this.

**Get ready, get set...**
Too many pets are purchased on impulse.  Only after buying a cute animal does the new owner ask what equipment and supplies are needed to take care of it.  This is a poor way to start.  A much better way is to first learn something about the needs of the animal you want.

Once you understand the needs of a hamster, you can then purchase the correct equipment and supplies—nothing extra. Remember, a pet store, like any other store, is in business to make a profit, and sometimes salespeople will suggest purchasing items that are not really necessary.

Before making any purchases, you'll have to decide if you are going to raise one hamster or two. Keeping both a male and a female, breeding them, and raising a family is fun and interesting, but there is also a lot to be said about having just *one* animal. It's easier to train one animal, and the cost of litter is less. All of your time can be spent with one pet, and finally, the part I like best—there is only one cage to clean.

Each hamster you purchase will require the following equipment: a cage, a cage cover, a waterer, an exercise wheel, and a few toys, which can be home-made. You will also need to keep your pet supplied with bedding (also known as litter) and food. You can, if you wish, add nesting material—some hamsters use it to make a soft bed.

Before buying your hamster, the equipment and supplies should be purchased, and the equipment should be taken home and washed with hot, soapy water, dried, and set up to make sure that everything works.

## Hamster housing

When choosing a cage, only consider one made of metal or glass. Pet shops do carry wooden and plastic cages, but a hamster can chew its way out of one of those in just a few hours.

Wire cages are lighter in weight and less expensive than glass cages, but they have one big drawback. The litter soon works its way through the bars and somehow gets scattered around the room. Also, it is not very pleasant watching an animal through wire bars.

A ten-gallon glass aquarium makes an ideal hamster home. It's heavier than a wire cage but not too heavy to handle. I weighed three different ten-gallon glass aquariums, and the average weight was a light eleven pounds.

A cage cover is needed more to keep other animals out than to keep the hamster in, although a hamster *can* jump. A mesh cover also helps prevent baby brothers or sisters from sticking their hands into the cage.

## The waterer

Desert animals, such as hamsters, need only a small amount of water, which they get from the green plants they eat. However, your hamster will be eating mostly dry pellets and dry seeds. It should be given lots of fresh water each day. I provide water for all of my animals, and they love it.

There are several different types of waterers, but most look and work about the same. They are simply containers which hang upside down from the top of the cage. At the bottom there is either a rubber or cork plug with a glass or metal tube running through it.

The glass tubes are small enough in diameter to allow one drop of water to hang at the drinking end. When the hamster laps up this drop, it's replaced by another. However, an air pocket sometimes forms in the narrow tube, preventing the water from flowing out. The metal tubes are larger in diameter—so large that the water would just run right through were it not that the drinking end is sealed by a metal ball. When the hamster pushes the ball up with either its teeth or its tongue, a drop of water comes out. Then the ball just reseats itself, sealing the tube. Since both types of waterers cost approximately the same, I recommend purchasing the type with the ball.

**Hamster workout**

A hamster needs a lot of exercise, and you'll need to give your pet some equipment for this. Wheel exercisers (as shown on page 13) are used within the cage

and work fine, although they sometimes make a squealing noise. (A drop of oil at each end of the axle usually solves the problem.) Wheel exercisers can be placed on the floor of the cage or hung from the sides.

There are also transparent plastic exercise balls for use outside the cage. Your hamster is entirely enclosed within the ball, which is placed on the floor. As the animal walks or runs, the ball rolls. The ball prevents the animal from hiding in tight spaces or gnawing on electric cords and electrocuting itself.

## Keeping a hamster happy

As I said before, an adult hamster will not tolerate another adult in its cage. But one animal in a cage with nothing to do soon becomes bored, and a bored animal spends most of its time sleeping. It's up to you to make life interesting for your pet! Talk to your hamster. Play with it. Train it. Give it toys to play with. *Don't expect the animal to entertain you. It's you who must entertain the animal.*

Pet shops carry toys for hamsters, but homemade toys will serve the purpose just as well. A clean, empty soup can, free of all sharp edges and with its paper label removed, will keep a hamster happy for hours, as will a piece of hard wood, such as a wooden clothespin, to chew on. Your hamster will think it's fun to hide under a piece of wood propped up at one end. Or if someone in your family is handy with tools, your pet will enjoy a simple wooden turntable or a box with a small hole to climb in and out of. Three or four toys are more than enough. Give your hamster one toy a day, but a different toy each day.

## The litter

Litter absorbs urine and any water that may spill from the waterer. A minimum of a half-inch of litter should be spread on the cage floor. You will soon see your hamster gather a pile of the litter into one corner to make a bed for itself.

A great many different types of material can be used: wood chips, wood shavings (with or without chlorophyll), coarse sawdust, cat litter, cocoa bean hulls (the room will smell of chocolate!), dried corncob pellets, sand, and dried grass or hay. Strong-smelling litter, such as cedar shavings, can cause irritation in the hamster's nose and throat. Pine shavings, which have less odor, are a better choice if you want to use wood shavings. Probably the material that absorbs best is dried corncob pellets. The worst absorbers are dried grass and cocoa hulls. But hamsters aren't fussy, and almost any litter is fine. I usually buy whatever is cheapest.

**What does a hamster eat?**
In a hamster's native habitat, its diet consists of plants, seeds, and an occasional insect. That's an easy diet to duplicate. Seed mixes for hamsters are available in one-pound boxes and in bulk from many pet stores. (Seed mixes put up for

finches and canaries are also suitable for hamsters. Some seed mixes for wild birds are also suitable, especially those mixes that contain only a few sunflower seeds. (Sunflower seeds are fattening.)

Some animal-feed companies grind seeds, add fillers, flavorings, vitamins, and minerals, and then press the mix into pellets of various sizes and shapes for different animals. Pellets for hamsters are usually sold in bulk or in one-pound boxes, and a one-pound box lasts for weeks when you have just one animal. One form of pelleted animal food—dog biscuits—can be purchased in almost any pet store. And yes, they are good for hamsters. Dog biscuits should not replace hamster pellets, but they make a good treat and help the rodents wear down their teeth.

Both seed mixes and pellets are nutritionally excellent, although hamsters tend to pick and choose their favorite seeds from the mixes, therefore not getting as complete a diet. Both are fed dry. Three large pellets can be put into your hamster's cage each day, and the animal will hide them, eating when it pleases. Or feed your pet half an ounce—about one tablespoon—of seeds in a heavy dish that cannot be easily turned over.

Every other day you can supplement your pet's diet by feeding it small pieces of lettuce, cabbage, carrot, celery, potato, apple, peach, pear, or other fruits and vegetables. Remove any uneaten fresh food after a few hours so that it doesn't spoil. Your hamster may hide some of it, so look through the litter.

Be careful not to feed your pet too much of these "wet" foods, especially when you first bring it home, as they can cause diarrhea. If you notice that your hamster has a runny bottom, stop feeding it the wet foods immediately.

You should never feed your hamster cookies, candy bars, or other sweet, oily foods. These can make a hamster sick.

If you feed your hamster seeds or pellets and give it pieces of fruits and vege-

tables, it is not necessary to feed it live insects. But hamsters do love them. If you want to give your animal insects, I recommend no more than one or two crickets per day. Only use crickets that come from a pet shop. Pet-shop crickets are raised to be fed to insect-eating animals and are free of all chemicals and pesticides that can harm your pet, while outdoor insects may be contaminated with all sorts of things. It's better to leave outdoor insects outdoors.

## Making a nest

Your hamster will build its own nest for sleeping. Many hamsters are quite content to make their nests from whatever kind of litter is supplied, but others like a softer bed. Nesting material is obtainable at pet shops, or you can do as I do and make your own. I use dried grass which I make from my lawn clippings. No pesticides or insecticides are used on my lawn, so I know the hay is safe. I place a handful of hay in the cage, and the hamster takes over. Some hamsters trample the hay to make a flat bed, others build a nest that looks very much like a bird's nest, and others just pile the hay loosely and then quickly disappear under the pile.

**No fleas, please!**

When the cage and other equipment are purchased, you should also buy a small can of flea spray. Read the label! It should say that the spray is made for use on mice, gerbils, hamsters, or even cats, but not for dogs. Flea sprays or powders made for dogs are too strong for small animals.

As a rule, hamsters don't have fleas, but store-bought hamsters are handled by clerks who touch a great many animals each day, and fleas may accidentally be transferred from one animal to another. You should control this problem right at the beginning.

Before bringing home your hamster, wash everything that your pet will come into contact with. This includes not only the cage, but the wire-mesh cage cover, the waterer, the exercise wheel, and any toys you buy or make. Be sure to rinse everything several times with clear water.

Then spray the four corners of the cage and the cage floor with flea spray. The instructions on the can may say that it is all right to spray an animal directly. You

may do so if you wish, but be careful not to get any in its eyes. Be sure the spray in the cage has dried, then place fresh litter on the floor, put water in the waterer, and seeds or pellets in the food dish. Add the exercise wheel and a toy or two.(Don't forget to wash your hands well after using the spray.)

Flea sprays do not kill fleas when they are in the egg stage. So, for the next four or five weeks, the cage should be resprayed each time it is cleaned.

20

If your pet appears to be scratching itself, remember, hamsters never need a bath. Like cats, they clean, brush, and comb themselves throughout the day, especially after waking and eating. This is done in a slow, relaxed manner. If your hamster looks irritated while grooming itself, there may be fleas or a skin problem. First treat for fleas. If this doesn't help, take the animal to a vet.

## Choosing a pet store

Let me tell you how I shop for new animals. I like to have plenty of time to visit two or even three pet stores before I do any buying. When I arrive at a new store, the first thing I do is ask one of the clerks or the manager a few simple questions about the animals I'm interested in. I may already know the answers, but I ask anyway to find out if anyone in the store is really knowledgeable. I like to shop in a store where I can go for help in case I run into a problem.

Also, I ask a clerk if I can handle one of the animals. I watch closely to see if the clerk treats the pets gently and with love or just as objects to be sold.

Finally, before leaving, I walk around the store to look at how clean it's kept. I especially check the puppy section. If their cages haven't been cleaned for several days, I walk out without buying anything. I'm willing to pay a bit more for an animal that comes from a well-run, clean store where the animals are taken care of in a loving way. I believe I will get a healthier, happier animal from such a store. Many people buy animals by price alone, but I think that is foolish.

## Decisions, decisions

When choosing your pet, look for a healthy animal that has a gentle disposition. Be wary of any hamster that has a poor coat, runny nose or eyes, or a wet bottom. These are all signs of trouble.

Both male and female hamsters make good pets. However, if all other factors

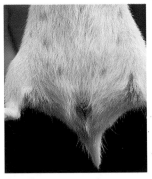

female                    male

such as color, price, and availability are equal, I would choose a male. I have found females to be a bit more aggressive, harder to train, and more likely to bite.

To tell male from female, pick up the hamster and check the location of the genitals in relation to its anus. In the male there is a space of about one-half inch. In the female the space is only about one-eighth inch. Also, the male's scrotum is quite noticeable.

More important than the sex of the animal is its age. Some shops sell baby hamsters as young as four weeks. A four-week-old hamster looks cute and is quite capable of taking care of itself. However, I've observed that when some hamsters this young are separated from their mother and siblings, they're not as friendly as those that have remained with their families until they are at least six weeks old.

A six-week- to ten-week-old hamster is much easier to train than a three-month- to six-month-old hamster. This doesn't rule out older hamsters. It just means that training older hamsters requires a bit more time and patience.

### Carrying home your prize

For carrying home small animals such as hamsters, my favorite pet shop places them in a thin paper box meant for canaries and parakeets. A hamster, if it has a mind to, can chew through a three-quarter-inch pine board in a few hours, and it can chew a hole through the thin paper box in just a few minutes. So when I go to the store, I bring with me a large empty metal can, such as a two-pound coffee can. I make sure that it is clean and free of all jagged edges. With a pencil, I punch six to eight air holes in the plastic lid.

I ask the clerk to place a handful of bedding in the can before putting the animal in. After checking to make sure that my new pet is comfortable, I place the lid on the can. Once the lid is on, I feel good knowing that my animal won't escape on its trip home. (Don't forget to bring one can for each hamster you plan to buy.)

Once home, I place the can on its side in the cage and let the animal walk out. Then I remove the can and place the wire-mesh cover on the cage. I watch the animal for a few minutes to make sure that it's all right, and then I leave the room. I would love to stay and play with my new pet, but it has just been through a rough experience. Leaving the animal alone at this point allows it to explore its

new environment. Tomorrow, or even the following day, it will feel more comfortable; then will be soon enough to begin our friendship.

## Getting to know your hamster

You can enjoy your hamster without ever touching it. Give your pet a toy, and it will play for hours. You'll have fun just watching. But it *is* fun to get more involved—to play with your animal and teach it tricks.

Making friends with a hamster, especially a young one, is easy. Each pet owner has a different way of getting to know an animal. I start by simply talking to it. I speak slowly and softly, alerting the animal to my presence. It soon learns that I am harmless. It also learns, very quickly, that I usually bring a goody.

Hamsters have a weakness for sunflower seeds, and a good seed mix always contains two or three per spoonful. Let the hamster enjoy the mix for a few days. From then on, remove the sunflower seeds and use them only as treats—bribes!

When you are ready to start training, select a big, fat sunflower seed and hold it between your thumb and forefinger. The hamster will slowly approach your fingers, then recoil at the smell of your hand. Continue offering it several times a day until the hamster finally takes the seed. Play this game over and over again until your pet fearlessly walks up to you for its treat.

Next, place several sunflower seeds on the palm of your hand and replay this game. It does take time, but if you don't give up, the day will come when your pet calmly sits on your hand eating a goody. Once this occurs, you can slowly lift the hamster out of the cage and play with it. (The safest way to pick up a hamster is by the scruff of its neck, but be especially careful not to drop your pet. It can be badly injured if it falls.)

To teach your pet to walk up your arm and sit on your shoulder, first place a seed or two on your wrist. After your hamster learns to walk across your hand to

your wrist, place the seed halfway between the wrist and elbow. Then put it on your elbow, and finally on your shoulder.

Never take your pet outdoors. Pet hamsters cannot stand direct sunlight or bad weather for very long. A good place to play with or to train your animal is on a bed so that if it should fall, it will fall only a short distance and onto something soft. It may walk to the very edge of the bed and look down, but chances are that it will never jump off. Still, it's always wise to close the door of the room. A closed door will keep other animals and people out, and if the hamster does jump off the bed, it will be confined to one room.

Should your hamster get loose, it will probably just walk around the room investigating everything. But keep in mind that hamsters like anything that looks like a tunnel. If your hamster crawls into a spot where your hand won't fit, try to bribe it out by placing an empty can, such as a coffee can, nearby. It might help to put some sunflower seeds in the can. Before long the hamster will crawl in. Once it is in the can, just cover the opening with your hand and transport the animal back to the bed or its cage. This is a good method to use whenever you need to move your hamster.

## To wake a sleeping hamster

Hamsters often sleep all day, but they don't mind getting up if you wake them correctly. Don't reach in and pick up a sleeping animal or make a lot of noise to wake it. You wouldn't like that—why should a hamster?

To wake a sleeping hamster, start by talking to it slowly and softly. After it stretches and yawns, give it a couple of sunflower seeds or a small piece of crisp lettuce. Once it's fully awake, you can take it out of its cage and play with it.

## Keeping house

Like it or not, cages must be cleaned. Hamster droppings are dry and odorless, but the urine does smell. Fortunately, a hamster will always urinate in the same corner. Remove the wet litter from that corner every day, using a large spoon. (If you have an aquarium cage, use a plastic spoon so you don't scratch the glass.) Add a little fresh litter to replace what you have removed. If you do this daily, a general cleaning is needed only once a week.

When you do the general cleaning, everything must be removed, washed, and dried. A good temporary home for the hamster is any tall container that has slippery walls, such as another aquarium, a plastic or metal pail, or a coffee can.

Dump the litter onto some newspapers or into a large grocery bag, and dispose of it in the garbage. Or you might put the litter in a compost pile so it can be used to fertilize the garden.

Wash and rinse the cage both inside and out. When it's dry, put in fresh litter, replace the food dish, exercise wheel, toys, and finally, the hamster.

If you are using bedding other than wood chips or shavings, you should also supply your animal with a wooden stick to chew on. Unlike the teeth of a human being, a hamster's teeth keep growing all its life. Compared to the teeth of mice and gerbils, a hamster's teeth grow slowly, but a hamster still needs to chew on something hard to keep its teeth worn and in shape. A hardwood stick about a half-inch in diameter and two or three inches long will do fine. Pet stores sell flavored sticks for this purpose, but a simple wooden clothespin does the job just as well and is a lot cheaper.

Because hamsters are desert animals, one might think they require a lot of sunshine, but this is not true. Remember that wild hamsters avoid the sun by sleeping in their burrows all day. Never place your pet's cage in direct sunlight for more than a few minutes. The cage, especially if covered, will not stay cool enough.

**A healthy hamster**

It's easy to tell when your hamster is healthy. Upon waking, a healthy hamster stretches and yawns. It may start its day by walking around the cage or eating or cleaning itself. It uses its exercise wheel often and likes to stand on its hind legs, checking out its environment. It has dry, non-smelly droppings, and its fur is smooth and shiny, with no bald spots.

A sick animal stays all curled up in one corner for long periods of time. Its droppings may be loose and smelly, and its rear end may be wet. Loose droppings and a wet rear end can be caused by a disease or by the overfeeding of fresh greens. If your animal has this problem, stop giving it fruits and vegetables for a few days and see if that helps. If not, talk to a veterinarian. Diarrhea can be a serious illness for a hamster.

If your animal seems to be sick, make a list of its symptoms and take the list to the pet shop. Pet stores carry a variety of medicines that are often quite effective. But if there is no noticeable improvement within a day or two, take the hamster to the veterinarian.

## Choosing to have pups

The question of whether you should mate your animals and start a hamster family is one that should be discussed with all members of your own family. I certainly don't recommend breeding animals time after time, but breeding hamsters once (and only once!) is both fascinating and educational.

The main problem, of course, is what to do with the babies when they grow up. An average litter consists of seven or eight youngsters. It may not be too difficult to find homes for seven cute, home-raised hamsters, but you should make arrangements before you begin the breeding process.

Don't assume you'll be able to give them to a pet shop. Pet shops like to get all their animals through their normal supplier. That way they know the animals will be healthy. But if you are unable to find homes for all your babies, ask a store owner. Most stores will accept a few pups from a customer. They usually won't pay you anything, but you may get a bag of pellets or seed in exchange.

If you have kept a male and a female for several months and they are still in good health and seem content, then you probably have the skill to breed them and take care of their youngsters. The only change in their care that I recommend is adding vitamin drops to the water. Pet shops have vitamin drops available, but I use the same kind that are fed to human babies. Start about one month before mating and continue the vitamins until the young are eight weeks old. You can stop feeding the drops to the male after the female has become pregnant.

I have bred many animals and raised many litters. Each litter has been interesting, and each has been different. The following set of photos is of one hamster family. The father's name is Fluffy, and the mother is called Rusty. Fluffy is a long-haired teddy-bear hamster. Rusty is a standard rusty-brown hamster. Both are about a year old. Hamsters can be bred as young as eight or nine weeks, but it is best to wait until they are at least four or even five months old.

## Mating your hamsters

Hamsters are very protective of their territory. If a male is placed in a female's cage, she will fight him to protect her territory. However, placing a female in with a male may or may not cause a fight, depending on how ready she is for breeding. I solve this problem a different way. I keep a third cage which is used only for breeding. Since neither hamster "owns" the breeding cage, there is less fighting.

Next to the breeding cage I keep a piece of stiff cardboard about eight inches by twelve inches. I use this to push between the two animals if they start to fight. *Never* reach in with your bare hands to separate fighting hamsters! Adults have teeth that are about one-half inch long, and they are razor sharp.

When a female is ready for mating, she is said to be "in heat" or "in season." Scientists have found that female hamsters are in season about every four days. One way to tell when a female is in season is to lightly stroke her back from her head to her tail. If she stands still, becomes stiff, and raises her short tail vertically, she is ready.

Using the coffee can method, transport the animals one at a time to the breeding cage. If the hamsters start to fight, push the cardboard between them, capture one of the animals in the coffee can, and return it to its cage. Then, still using the can, gather the second hamster and take it back to its home. Remember that even after you remove one of the hamsters, the remaining animal is still worked up and ready to fight. Be careful. Use the can, not your hands.

If the female shows signs of being in heat and yet fights with the male, the timing may not be just right. It may be a bit early or late. The only way to find out is to try breeding them again in about six or eight hours. If they still fight, you will have to try again in a few days when the female next shows signs of coming into heat.

If the female is in heat and receptive to breeding, she will at first ignore the male. He will chase after her, nudge her, lick her head and ears, and sniff her genitals. (She also may sniff his.) She may remain motionless for a few moments and then move on; he will follow, and the nudging, licking, and sniffing will start all over again. After a few minutes, if everything goes well, her body stiffens. He will then raise her hindquarters with his nose and begin copulation (mating). This lasts only a few seconds, but the hamsters can copulate over and over again for the next forty to sixty minutes.

Don't leave the breeding cage! Stay right there the full forty to sixty minutes. At any time the female may get tired and call it quits. When she does, the animals will either separate and go to opposite sides of the cage to wash themselves, or the female will attack the male. If she attacks, use the cardboard to separate the two, as the female can easily injure or kill her mate. Once again, use the coffee can to take your hamsters to separate cages.

## Preparing for the new family

Successful mating doesn't automatically mean the female is going to have a litter. Fluffy and Rusty were mated three times before Rusty became pregnant. It's so hard to tell if the female is pregnant that you may not know until you see the babies! Since there is often a surplus of food in the cage, you may not notice that she is eating more. She will put on some weight and become wider, but these are such gradual changes you may not see them. If she has a coat of short hair, she may look lumpy the last day or two, but if she has long hair, even late pregnancy is not obvious. She will continue with all of her normal activities—eating, sleeping, playing, and exercising. Her gestation period (the time it takes for the babies to grow enough to be born) lasts between sixteen and eighteen days. At the end of that period, you may observe your mother-to-be busily building a nest. She may prepare her nest only hours before giving birth.

There really is not much you can do to get the pregnant female ready for the birth process, other than to clean her cage on the fifteenth day after mating and give her some nesting material. Once the babies are born, try not to touch the mother or babies, or even empty the cage litter, for about two weeks.

Most animal mothers are protective of their newborns. If they feel threatened, many will be so upset they will kill their young. Hamster mothers can do this, so it's best not to disturb the family. However, if the mother doesn't object, you can continue gently scooping out the urine-soaked litter from the corner of the cage. Supply her with fresh vitamin-enriched water each day, and place her food in a corner opposite the nest so she will get off the nest and walk about.

## The birth of the pups

If you want to see the birth of the pups, you will have to check on the mother-to-be every hour or so, day and night, beginning on the sixteenth day after mating.

If you happen to be present for the birth, I'm afraid that you might be disappointed. While birth is a thrilling and awesome event, it's hard to see the baby hamsters as they emerge from the underside of their mother. Each unborn baby develops within a sac containing a waterlike fluid. As soon as the pup is born, the mother tears open this sac with her teeth and washes the newborn, cleaning it and stimulating its breathing. Then the mother eats the sac. (Many animal mothers eat the birth sac.) As the babies are born, you may notice some blood. Do not be concerned. This is normal.

Rusty's second pup was born thirty-eight minutes after the first. This is an unusually long time. In fact, after a half-hour had gone by, I put my camera away, assuming that the litter was going to consist of only one pup. Then the second one came, and three minutes later, the third. At this point the mother was so busy with the two new arrivals that I was able to steal the first pup from her, photograph it, and replace it before she missed it. By the time the seventh baby was born, pups were scattered all over the floor of the cage. Adult hamsters seldom make any sounds. Their babies, on the other hand, are quite noisy.

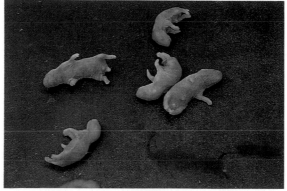

This was Rusty's third litter, yet she was baffled. She did not seem to know what to make of all the babies or what to do with them. She would pick up one in her mouth, carry it for awhile, and then just drop it.

To take the pictures for this book, I did something that you should *not* do. Just before the start of the birthing, I moved Rusty to a special cage with a dull, black floor that would not reflect my flash. About an hour after the seventh pup was born, I decided that she was finished and that it was time to move everyone back to her cage. I made a nest in the corner by forming a hollow in the bedding with my fist. The babies were moved first, one by one, and then the mother.

All was well for a few moments. The mother checked the babies, walked around re-inspecting her cage, drank some water, walked back to the nest, picked up a baby, and while I watched with horror, *ate it!* She then picked up a second one and swallowed it as well! *As I watched, she ate all seven pups!*

Strangely, though the pups had been very vocal earlier, not a sound came from a single one as it was being eaten. After pup number six had been swallowed, I noticed that Rusty's cheek pouches were enlarged. She *wasn't* eating the pups after all! She was placing them in her cheek pouches so she could move them. And move them she did. She spit one out here and one out there—one even fell

birthday photo

into the seed dish. I then picked up all seven and placed them back in the nest, and this time she let them be. It was now past midnight. I had had enough. I turned the lights out and called it a day.

I have since learned that hamsters will carry their young in their cheek pouches if they feel that they or their babies are in danger. Rusty was probably scared because I had moved her from cage to cage and had handled her babies.

**The Family Diary**

THE PUPS' FIRST DAY:   Before I had breakfast, I checked on the mother and babies to see if everything was okay. From previously observing Rusty with her families, I knew that she liked to build her own nests, so I placed a big handful of dry, loose hay at the far side of the cage. Rusty had to leave her babies to get the hay. This gave me the opportunity to remove a pup, weigh it, and photograph it. Its weight: 3.4 grams, just a bit more than a penny!

She decided to build her nest over her babies, which were still in the hollow that I had created with my fist. Rusty was so busy fetching hay and building that she didn't notice when I replaced the pup.

35

I didn't bother Rusty the rest of the day. I just placed a few extra pellets in the cage because nursing mothers need to eat a little more than usual.

TWO DAYS OLD: The pups may be only two days old, but they are amazingly strong. This one squeaks and squirms, and it is tricky for me to hold it while I take its picture. Rusty makes no effort to look for her pup.
  During the first few days of life, hamster pups spend all of their time either sleeping or nursing. Rusty is with them constantly, only getting up to make brief trips to her food dish and waterer.

FOUR DAYS OLD: The pups begin moving about rapidly now, with a swimming sort of motion. Their whiskers are developing, with hairs growing up, down, side-ways, backwards, and forwards. These whiskers, along with the pups' sense of smell, help the babies find their way back to the nest when they fall out.

SIX DAYS OLD: The moment Rusty leaves the nest, one of the pups slips away, and using only its sensitive whisker hairs (its eyes are still closed), explores the cage without bumping into a single object.

SEVEN DAYS OLD: First tooth!

two days old

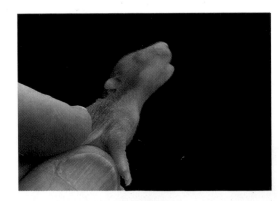

36

NINE DAYS OLD: Even with four teeth, the pups continue to nurse and will do so for another few days. (This must be painful for Rusty.) However, they do not nurse as often as they did when they were first born. A few begin using their front paws like hands, picking up various items and tasting them. It is now time to scatter seeds, pellets, and a few dog biscuits on the floor of the cage where the pups can get at them. You don't need to give them much food; one or two pellets and a spoonful of seeds should be enough. If you listen carefully, you may actually hear their tiny teeth grinding away bits of pellets or dog biscuits.

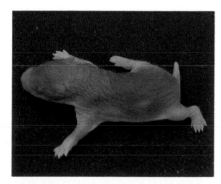

four days

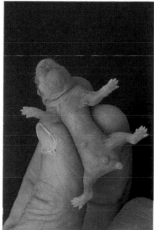

four days

nine days

six days

37

TEN DAYS OLD: As soon as Rusty carries one pup back to the nest, another leaves. Her children are growing fast. This one is six centimeters long (about two and one-half inches)—about one-and-a-half times its birth size. Some sexual characteristics are developing. The nipples on this female are visible.

TWELVE DAYS OLD: There are no hard and fast rules, but you can try adding soft greens as well as some hard vegetables to the pups' diet at about this age. Rusty's pups began to enjoy eating carrots.

Once the pups stop nursing, it's time to lower the waterer so both mother and young can reach it.

The pup on page 40 is enjoying its first carrot.

You can begin handling the young hamsters when they are about two weeks old. Let them become accustomed to you slowly, just as your adult hamster did.

ten days

ten days

twelve days

twelve days

SEVENTEEN DAYS OLD: In seven days the pups have grown almost an inch. This one is eight centimeters long (about three and one-fourth inches).

They're all over the cage, but Rusty doesn't give up. She tries and tries to keep her children in the nest, but they have minds of their own.

THREE WEEKS OLD: Now the eyes of all the babies are open, and they are ready for toys—not just one toy, but many. They will soon be bored with just one toy, so if you have only two toys, alternate them. A good toy can be as simple as a clean, empty tin can or the lid from a smaller aquarium placed in the cage at an angle good for climbing.

Pet shops have many colorful toys, such as exercise wheels *without spokes* for use when there are several animals in the cage. (An exercise wheel with spokes, such as shown on page 13, must be removed once the pups are tall enough to touch it. The pups can get caught in the wheel if they try to climb on it while it's

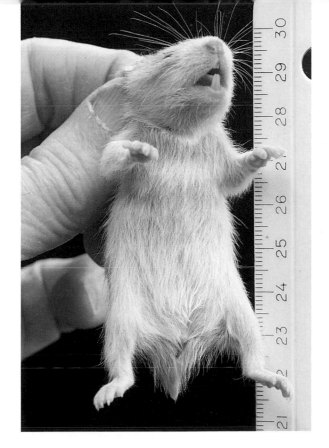

seventeen days—
eight centimeters long

in use. Only one animal should be in the cage with such a wheel.) Look for interesting, safe toys such as the house with doors for coming and going, shown on page 42. Cans and tubes are fun; hamsters just love going in and out of them.

FOUR WEEKS OLD: The babies are all grown up. Some commercial breeders deliver them to the pet stores at this age, but I find they make better pets if they stay with their litter-mates another week or so.

They're still great friends. If one eats, they all want to eat. If one sleeps, they all want to sleep. If one decides it wants to chew on a new stick, they all want to chew. And just like some human siblings, they like roughing it up.

41

three weeks

four weeks

I measure and weigh them for the last time. They average ten centimeters long (about four inches) and weigh a little over three ounces. Their eyes, ears, and teeth are well developed, and it is now easy to tell the males from the females. However, they still have the dull coloring of juveniles. Their coats will gradually get brighter over the next month.

FIVE WEEKS OLD: The mother and the babies still get along just fine in one cage, but the babies are no longer babies. They are sexually mature, and the males and females should be placed in separate cages. There have been times when I was busy and did not separate my young hamsters. Soon my seven-week- to eight-week-old babies had babies!

By now, you should have found good homes for all your pups. If not, separate them and start looking. If homes are not found, you'll have to set up more cages and buy more food. Remember to continue playing with and handling the young hamsters each day. This will make training them that much easier for their next owners.

## When a hamster dies

There comes a time when all living things, plant and animal, die. Even though death is a part of life, it hurts when a pet you care about dies. There is nothing wrong about feeling sad and crying when you have to say goodbye to your lovely pet hamster. Each person, each family, each religion, and each culture has different ideas and feelings about dying and death. Talking with your family about death makes dealing with the loss of a pet easier.

## Photographing your hamster family

Would you like to photograph your hamsters? It's not too difficult.

Taking portraits is especially easy. Simply have someone hold the animal near a sunny window (but not directly in front of the window), move in close with your camera, and shoot away. Depending on how close you can focus your camera, you can either shoot both the person and the hamster or the hamster by itself.

Doing life history studies is a bit more difficult but more rewarding. I believe that studies of an animal—any animal—should be done with the animal living in its normal environment. That means you should photograph your hamster in its aquarium house.

The biggest problem is the four glass walls of the aquarium, which not only allow us to see the animal but everything that's behind and to the sides of the aquarium as well. Your hamster may be lost in the photo's background. Also, under certain conditions, glass acts like a mirror, reflecting everything that is in front of it. I will help you solve these problems by passing on some trade secrets—if you promise not to tell others how you produced your beautiful photographs!

Cover the inside of the back and side walls of the aquarium with something you can't see through, such as a towel or piece of cardboard. The covering will stop all reflections from these three walls and separate your hamster, visually, from the many things behind the aquarium. Try to use a covering that is darker or lighter than your animal.

Clean the front wall both inside and out. Place the aquarium so that this wall faces away from windows, white walls, or any light-colored object. In addition,

you must wear dark clothing, and if possible, use a camera that has no chrome trimming. There should be nothing facing the front of the aquarium that could be reflected by the glass.

Not every camera lends itself to this type of photography. Many auto-focus cameras must be switched from auto focus to manual focus because the camera will automatically focus on the glass and not on the hamster.

Built-in flash units cannot be used because the glass will reflect the flash. Try using a portable flash unit. Aim it at a forty-five-degree angle to the front wall of the aquarium or aim it at the ceiling to get soft, even illumination.

Finally, many camera lenses, especially zoom lenses, can focus no closer than three to five feet. This is not close enough to give you a large image of your hamster. One solution is to buy a set of three close-up lenses, sometimes called "portrait lenses." These screw onto the front of your present lens and allow you to get closer to your subject, producing a larger image on the film. Be sure to take your camera *and lens* with you when buying these, for they come in many sizes.

Films with low ASA/ISO numbers, such as 25 or 64, produce color prints which have the best color. However, unless you have a very powerful electronic flash unit, it's best to purchase faster film with ASA/ISO numbers of 400 or 1,000.

If your school has a camera club, perhaps you can join and learn how to improve your skills. Keep shooting, have fun, and good luck with your hamster and your photography!

# Index

babies, 29, 32-37, 39-41, 43-44
bedding, 13, 14, 16-17, 19, 20, 23, 27, 32, 34
birthing, 32-35
birth sac, 33
breeding, 11, 13, 29-32
buying hamsters, 5-6, 11-13, 21-23
cage, 13, 14, 16, 20, 23, 27-28, 30-31, 32, 34,
    40-41, 43, 44, 45, 46
cage cleaning, 12, 13, 20, 27, 32, 45
cheek pouches, 8, 11, 34-35
chewing, 14, 16, 18, 23, 27-28
Chinese (dwarf) hamster, 11
coloring, 11
common hamster, 11
death, 44
diarrhea, 18, 21, 28
diet, 9, 11, 14, 17-19, 27, 28, 29, 32, 36, 37,
    39
dwarf (Chinese and Siberian) hamster, 11
equipment, 12-13, 14-16, 20
exercise, 15-16, 32
exercise ball, 16
exercise wheel, 13, 15-16, 20, 27, 28, 40-41
fathers, 29
females, 7, 13, 21-22, 30-31
fighting, 30-31
fleas, 20-21
golden (Syrian) hamster, 6, 11, 29
grooming, 21, 28
handling, 9, 22-23, 24, 25, 27, 30-31
health, 12, 21, 28, 29
illness, 18, 21, 28
insects, as food, 19

life span, 11
long-haired (teddy bear) hamster, 11, 29
males, 7, 13, 21-22, 29-31, 43
mammals, 6
mating, 30-31, 32
mothers, 6, 29, 32-37, 39-40, 43
natural environment, 9, 11, 14, 17, 28
nesting material, 13, 19, 32, 35
nursing, 36, 37, 39
pelleted feed, 14, 18, 20, 29, 36, 37
pet store, 5, 11-14, 16-19, 21-23, 28, 29,
    40, 41
photography, 33-36, 44-46
play, 9, 16, 23-25, 27, 32, 40-41, 44
pregnancy, 32
rodents, 6, 18
seed mix, 14, 17-18, 20, 24-25, 27, 29, 37
sex, distinguishing, 22, 39, 43
short-haired hamster, 11
Siberian (dwarf) hamster, 11
size, 7, 11, 39, 40, 43
sleep cycle, 9, 27, 36
smell, sense of, 7, 24, 36
Syrian golden hamster, 6, 11, 29
teddy bear (long-haired) hamster, 11, 29
teeth, 6, 18, 27-28, 30, 33, 36, 37, 43
tetanus, 12
touch, sense of, 7, 36, 37
toys, 13, 16, 20, 24, 27, 40-41
training, 13, 16, 22, 24-25, 44
veterinarian, 12, 21, 28
vitamins, 29, 32
waterer, 13, 14-15, 16, 20, 36, 39
weight, 7, 35, 43

**About the Author**  Jerome Wexler was introduced to photography by his ninth-grade science teacher in an after-school camera club. He has been a professional photographer since 1946 and has had approximately fifteen thousand photographs published all over the world.

Mr. Wexler's photos have always been used for educational purposes. He first worked as an agricultural photographer, taking pictures of all kinds of farming activities as well as good and bad farming practices. The photos were used in advertisements, farm journals, magazines, and textbooks.

What he loves to do most is illustrate—with photographs—children's books on plants, animals, and insects. *Pet Hamsters* is his forty-second such book. Many have received honors and awards; some have been translated and republished in Japan, China, Germany, Finland, Sweden, Holland, and Great Britain.

Both the Smithsonian Institution and the Agricultural Photo Library, a division of the United States Department of Agriculture, have asked Mr. Wexler to consider leaving them his vast collection of thirty-seven thousand photographs.